I0436067

Number ONE World Facts

Copyright © 2013 by TheBrothers.
All Rights reserved.
Any part of this book may be used or
reproduced in any matter whatsoever without
permission in writing from the author except in
the case of brief quotations embodied in critical
articles or review.
First Edition ,2013

We would like to say

Thank You

for buying this book.

Go into the following url address :

http://amazon4u.ravpage.co.il/worldfactsthankyou

and get a FREE Gift (Yes i! It's FREE)

ABOUT THIS BOOK

" Knowledge is a familiarity with someone or something, which can include facts, information, descriptions, or skills acquired through experience or education " *Wikipedia*.

As parents we want the best for our children.

This book is about acquiring knowledge. We wrote this book in a very unique, fun and interesting way in order to enable you, as a parent, to read, learn and explain these new facts to your children.

It took us a long time and a lot of effort to investigate, discover and bring you the most interesting and amazing facts.

Each book includes a different number which is associated with facts that contain this number, as we said before, it is unique.

Read the book to your children speaks to them about it and explain it to them.

Enjoy!

We live on planet Earth and we have only *one* of it.

Did you know that?
If we could shrink the Earth to the size of a billiard ball it would
 be just as smooth as a billiard ball.

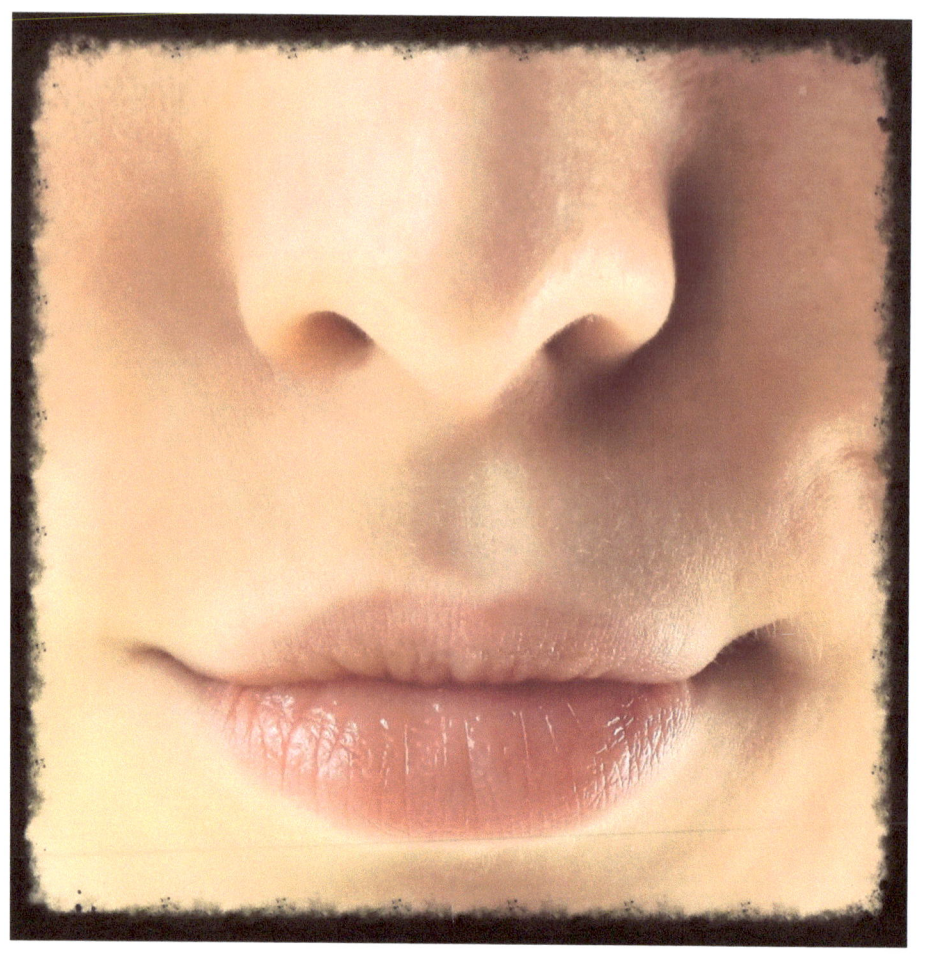

Humans have *one* nose, *one* head, *one* tongue, *one* mouth and *one* heart.

Did you know that?
Even though our noses can sense lots of different smells dog's noses are far more sensitive to smells than ours.

Although Earth is covered by five oceans there is only *one* Atlantic Ocean.

Did you know that?
The oceans are so big that they cover over 71% of the Earth's surface.
The names of the Earth's five oceans are: the Pacific Ocean, the Atlantic Ocean, the Indian Ocean, the Arctic Ocean and the Southern Ocean.

Cyclops were mythological creatures that only had *one* eye which was in the middle of their foreheads.

Did you know that?
Cyclopes were huge monsters in Greek mythology. Greek Mythology is a collection of stories and myths created by the ancient Greeks - in ancient times the Greeks based their spiritual and religious beliefs on these stories.

In just one night *one* mole can dig a 300 feet long tunnel.

Did you know that?
If you were to dig a hole right through the earth from any point in the United States you would find yourself in the Indian Ocean on the other side.

You could save enough energy to watch TV for 3 hours by recycling just *one* glass jar.

Did you know that?
Energy is what makes things happen, it is what makes people, plants and even machines work, it also makes the sun, the moon and stars shine.

If you were living in Germany and Austria you would be happy

to take home a test with a "*one*" on it, because it would mean "very good".

Did you know that?
The design of the Austrian flag is so old that it is thought to be one of the oldest flags in the world.

The letters in the number "*one*" are in reverse alphabetical order.

Did you know that?
The oldest known object containing tally notches is the Ishango bone. It was discovered in the Congo and is 22,000 years old.
This bone is the oldest calculator in the world.

We have *one* father, *one* mother and *one* family.

Did you know that?
The Chinese philosopher and educator Confucius is said to have the longest family tree in the world. The tree covers over 80 generations and includes more than 2 million family members, he was a descendant of King Tang.

There is more vitamin C in *one* - third of a pound of broccoli stalk than in 204 apples.

Did you know that?
Humans, guinea pigs, fruit bats and gorillas are the only mammals that need to ingest vitamin C, most animals make their own vitamin C.

Our universe has more than a hundred billion galaxies and each *one* has billions of stars

Did you know that?
Even though the stars we see in the sky at night seem like a tiny dot of light most of them are actually two star systems.

Yelling for 8 years, 7 months and 6 days straight would give you enough energy to heat *one* cup of coffee.

Did you know that?
Dogs' hearing is different to humans'; they hear at a different frequency meaning that they can hear some noises that we don't hear.

The Indus blind dolphin, which is found in the Indus and Ganges rivers in South Asia is born blind and has a highly sophisticated sonar system. These dolphins are also known as side-swimming dolphins because they swim on *one* side.

Did you know that?
Dolphins are very intelligent animals, they communicate with each other in their own language made up of clicks, whistles and other sounds?

One raindrop is made up of one million cloud droplets.

Did you know that?
Water evaporates into the sky and condenses in the cold air forming clouds.

Grapefruits grow in clusters like grapes, hence their name.

One cluster can contain up to 25 grapefruits.

Did you know that?
Grapefruits were first reported to be grown in Barbados, a Caribbean island, and today they are grown in many countries.

In New Zealand you will find a lizard called the tuatara lizard which has three eyes, two in the middle of its head and *one* on top of its head.

Did you know that?
If you catch a lizard its tail might fall off its body.

When flamingos fly they can reach a speed of approximately 55 kilometers an hour. They can travel about 600 km in *one* night.

Did you know that?
Flamingo birds are named for the bright color of their feathers and the origin of the name is "flamenco" which is the Spanish word for fire?

A honey bee visits about 75 flowers in *one* collecting trip.

Did you know that?
Honey is the only food produced by an insect (the honey bee) that human's eat.

Chameleons can move their eyes in different directions simultaneously.

One eye can be looking forward and *one* eye backward at the same time.

Did you know that?
Chameleons most often change from green to brown and back but some can also turn to other colors and it only takes 20 seconds for this change to occur.

Sharks have the ability to detect a *one* drop of blood from very far away.

Did you know that?

Sharks have many rows of teeth, if they lose one tooth another moves forward and replaces it – one shark may grow and use over 20, 000 teeth in its lifetime.

They say that Leonardo da Vinci could write with

one hand

and draw with the other simultaneously.

Did you know that?
The Mona Lisa, Leonardo da Vinci's famous painting, is hanging in the Louvre in France? It has its own room which is climate controlled and the painting is covered with bullet proof glass.

(Wait ... there is more on the next page)

Did you like this book??

Take *one* Min and give us an Honest Review.

It's Important to us.

We have more "*Number Facts Series*"

Amazon Link :

http://www.amazon.com/dp/B00G8BBBJ4

http://www.amazon.com/dp/B00GGNB3W4

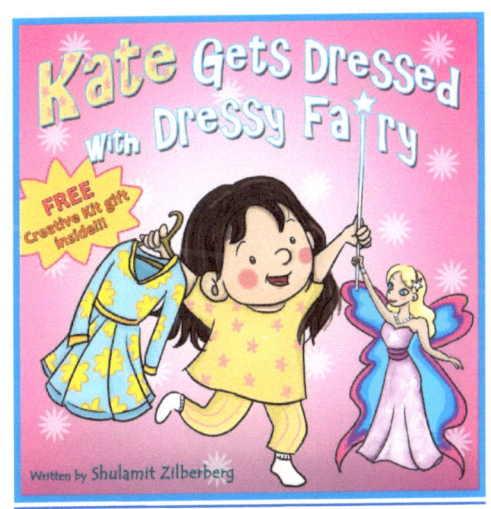

http://www.amazon.com/dp/B00GTMQ2FU

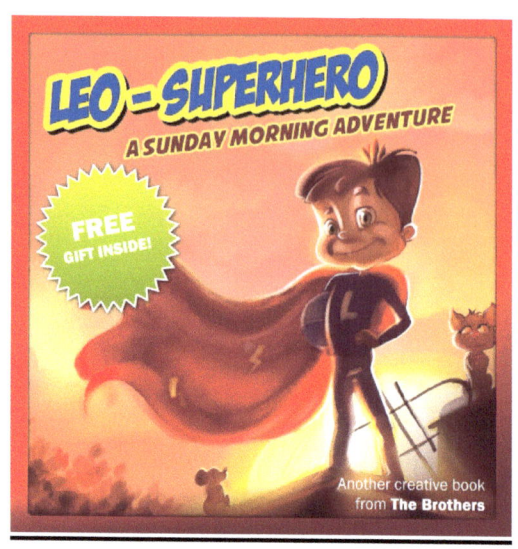

http://www.amazon.com/dp/B00EUX4C70

http://www.amazon.com/dp/ B00FB6M902

www.ingramcontent.com/pod-product-compliance
Lightning Source LLC
Chambersburg PA
CBHW050928290526
45792CB00002B/925